(*The Classic Collection*)

WITHDRAWN

·ELEGANT·
AFGHANS

KC PUBLISHING, INC.

700 West 47th Street, Suite 310 • Kansas City, Missouri 64112

COPYRIGHT 1996 KC PUBLISHING, INC.

All rights reserved. No part of this work may be reproduced without written permission from the publisher, except by a reviewer who may quote short passages in a review with appropriate credits.

Instructions have been carefully checked for accuracy. The publisher, however, cannot be responsible for human error, misinterpretation of directions or the differences of individual needleworkers.

Attention Schools and Business Firms:
KC PUBLISHING books are available at quantity discounts for bulk purchases for education, business or sales promotion use. For more information call our Book Department at (816) 531-5730.

Printed in the United States of America

ELEGANT AFGHANS

ISBN: 0-86675-347-8

ELEGANT AFGHANS

TABLE OF CONTENTS

Lacy Granny Ripple *Crochet*	16	Christmas Tree Afghan *Crochet*	62
Patchwork Baby Doll Afghan *Knit*	20	American Flag Afghan *Crochet*	66
Tulip Baby Afghan *Knit*	22	Olympic Rings Afghan *Crochet*	70
Hearts & Flowers Afghan *Crochet*	24	Blue Diamond Afghan *Crochet*	76
Big, Bold Beautiful Diamond Afghans *Crochet / Knit*	28	Soft, Warm and Gray Afghan *Knit*	82
Seascape Afghan *Crochet*	36		

USEFUL INFORMATION

Storytime Afghan *Knit*	40	Introduction	2
		Abbreviations & Terms	3
Sunday Afternoon Afghan *Crochet*	44	Helpful Hints	4
		Reference Guide for Crocheters	6
Popcorn Party Afghan *Crochet*	48	Color Photos of Patterns	7
Hearts Afire Afghan *Knit*	52	Reference Guide for Knitters	15
Sweetheart Afghan *Crochet*	58	Index	85

```
746.43 El  Large Print
Elegant afghans /
```

449 5959

INTRODUCTION

Afghans continue to be among the most requested patterns of knitters and crocheters. Just what makes a coverlet of yarn so popular?

Afghans, worked in colors to complement a room, are often used as decorating accents. Attractive draped on the back of a couch, an afghan is also highly practical for comfy reclining with a good book or enjoying a favorite video.

Because afghan patterns almost always repeat rows or rounds of the design many times in succession, they are easy to work without constantly referring back to the pattern. It's easy to work on an afghan while riding in the car, talking on the telephone, or watching television. Knitters and crocheters usually find it hard to sit still unless their hands are busy and working — an afghan is the perfect occupation for restless fingers.

A handmade afghan is a wonderful gift — sure to be used often and treasured for years. Whether for a brand new baby, a college student going away from home for the first time, a new home owner, or a retiree, an afghan is the perfect way to let loved ones know they are special. You can be sure the recipient will think of you often, in the most pleasant of circumstances, when they are snuggled under the warm folds of your creation.

This book contains patterns of simple to challenging patterns but the results are all sure to be stunningly elegant. Happy knitting and crocheting!

Executive Editor

ELEGANT AFGHANS

ABBREVIATIONS AND TERMS

Crochet

bl	block stitch	p	picot
CC	Contrasting Color	pc	popcorn stitch
ch(s)	chain(s)	rnd	round
cl	cluster	sc	single crochet
dc	double crochet	sk	skip
dec	decrease	sl st	slip stitch
dtr	double treble crochet	sp(s)	space(s)
hdc	half double crochet	st	stitch
inc	increase	tr	treble crochet
lp	loop	tr tr	treble treble crochet
MC	Main Color	yo	yarn over

Knit

CC	Contrasting Color	rnd	round
dec	decrease	sk	skip
inc	increase	sl	slip
K	knit	sp	space
lp	loop	st	stitch
MC	Main Color	tbl	through back loop
P	purl	tog	together
psso	pass slip stitch over	yo	yarn over

Gauge — The number of stitches to the inch horizontally and the number of rows to the inch vertically.

Work Even — Continue working the pattern without increasing or decreasing the row length by adding or omitting any stitches.

HELPFUL HINTS

YARN

Always purchase an extra amount of yarn in the same dye lot. If it is not needed, most shops will give you credit for any unused full balls.

Ply does not determine weight or thickness of yarn. Ply denotes the number of individual yarns twisted together to make a single strand. The thickness depends on the diameter of the yarn — some being very fine, others very bulky.

GAUGE

The most important way to make your project the correct size is to check your gauge. Remember — TO SAVE TIME, TAKE TIME TO CHECK GAUGE. Your own knitting/crocheting tension may require different needle or hook sizes than those given in instructions to achieve the correct stitch gauge.

Hooks and needles recommended for different weights of yarns are: baby-weight, D hook and number 3 needles; sport-weight, F-G hook and number 5 needles; worsted-weight, H-J hook and number 8-10 needles; bulky-weight, K hook and number 10-13 needles.

YARN OVERS

Yarn overs can be confusing for both beginning and experienced knitters. Those yarn overs that are most confusing are the ones occuring between knit and purl stitches. To yarn over after a purl stitch, before a knit stitch, move yarn over right-hand needle and knit next stitch in usual manner. To yarn over after a knit stitch, before a purl stitch, move yarn to front (towards you) between the needles, over right-hand needle and back to the front again. Purl the next stitch.

JOINING YARN WHEN KNITTING

When you need to start a new skein of yarn, start a new color or cut out a bad place in the yarn, there are three proven methods of joining. The best way is to drop the end of yarn at the beginning of a row, leaving about a two-inch length, and begin working with the new yarn, leaving about a two-inch length. After the article is finished, thread the yarn ends in a blunt needle and weave them in and out for eight or ten stitches.

You may also join yarn at the end of a row by making a slipknot with the new strand around the previous strand. Draw slipknot close to end of work.

Another method is to work within four inches of end of yarn, then lay a new strand along the old so that about one inch extends beyond last stitch. Knit the four inches with double yarn, cutting the ends after completion of piece.

JOINING YARN WHEN CROCHETING

To start new yarn or a new color, work a stitch up to the last step, pick up the new yarn and complete the last step of the stitch. Keep both loose ends on the wrong side to be woven into the piece later.

CHANGING COLORS WHEN KNITTING

When changing from one color to the next in the middle of a knit row (or anywhere between the two ends, for that matter), twist one color of yarn around the other. The twist should show up on the wrong side of the work. Weave in and trim loose ends later. Neglecting to twist yarn ends around each other at a color change will result in a hole or gap in the work.

Horizontal stripes are easier because color changes are always made at the beginning of a row.

ELEGANT AFGHANS
REFERENCE GUIDE FOR CROCHETERS

SINGLE CROCHET

Chain desired number of stitches. Insert hook from front under top two strands of second chain from hook.

Yarn over the hook and draw through stitch (two loops on hook).

Yarn over hook again and draw through two loops (one loop remains on hook, one single crochet made).

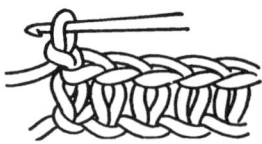

Insert hook under top two strands of yarn on next stitch and repeat previous steps until a single crochet has been made in every stitch of chain; then chain one stitch for turning.

DOUBLE CROCHET

Chain desired number of stitches. Yarn over and insert hook from front under top two strands of fourth chain from hook.

Yarn over again and draw through stitch (three loops on hook).

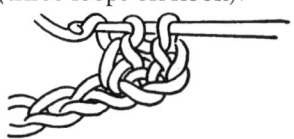

Yarn over again and draw through first two loops (two loops remain on hook).

Yarn over and draw through two loops (one loop remains, one double crochet made).

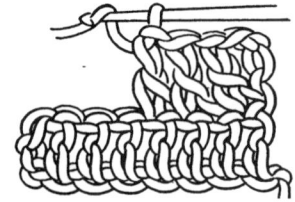

*Yarn over, insert hook in next ch and draw up a loop, yarn over and pull through two loops, yarn over and pull through two loops. Repeat from * until a double crochet has been made in every stitch of chain; then chain three for turning.

ELEGANT AFGHANS

Lacy Granny Ripple *(Crochet)* — Page 16

Patchwork Baby Doll Afghan *(Knit)* — page 20

Tulip Baby Afghan (*Knit*) page 22

Hearts & Flowers Afghan (*Crochet*) page 24

ELEGANT AFGHANS

Big, Bold Beautiful Diamond Afghans *(Crochet and Knit)* — page 28

Seascape Afghan *(Crochet)* — page 36

Storytime Afghan *(Knit)* page 40

Sunday Afternoon Afghan *(Crochet)* page 44

Popcorn Party Afghan *(Crochet)* page 48

Hearts Afire Afghan *(Knit)* page 52

ELEGANT AFGHANS

page 58

Sweetheart Afghan *(Crochet)*

American Flag Afghan *(Crochet)*

page 66

Christmas Tree Afghan *(Crochet)* page 62

Olympic Kings Afghan *(Crochet)* page 70

ELEGANT AFGHANS

Blue Diamond Afghan (*Crochet*) page 76

Soft, Warm and Gray Afghan (Knit) page 62

14

ELEGANT AFGHANS
Reference Guide for Knitters

KNITTING A STITCH

Hold needle with cast on stitches in left hand, insert empty needle held in right hand into first stitch on left needle. With yarn at back of work, bring it under and then over right needle point.

Draw newly-formed loop through stitch on left needle.

This newly-formed stitch remains on the right needle. Work into each stitch in the same manner until all stitches have been transferred to the right needle.

PURLING A STITCH

Hold needle with cast on stitches in left hand, insert empty needle from back to front of first stitch on left needle. With yarn at front of work, bring it over and around right needle point.

Draw newly-formed loop through stitch on left needle.

This newly-formed stitch remains on the right needle. Work into each stitch in the same manner until all stitches have been transferred to the right needle.

ELEGANT AFGHANS

Shown in color on page 7

LACE GRANNY RIPPLE

Who said afghans were only good for cold winter nights? This sweet, soft cover-up is specially suited for spring and summer days (or nights). Perfect for lazy afternoons in the shade by

CROCHET

the lake, this afghan will make book-reading or daydreaming time extra comfortable when a cool breeze suddenly blows.

Materials: Worsted weight acrylic yarn in the following colors and amounts: 7 skeins (3.5 ounce skeins containing approximately 260 yards) light rose (MC) and 3 skeins light green (CC); tapestry needle; and a size K crochet hook.

Finished Measurements: Approximately 42 inches x 56 inches

Gauge: To work gauge and try out pattern, ch 39 and work Rows 1-5. This swatch should measure 10 inches wide.

TO SAVE TIME, TAKE TIME TO CHECK GAUGE.

Special Abbreviation:
Shell — (3 dc, ch 2, 3 dc) in st.

With MC ch 159.

ROW 1 Dc in 4th ch from hook and in next ch, ch 1, sk next ch, dc in each of next 3 ch, ch 1, sk next ch, shell in next ch, ch 1, sk next ch, dc in each of next 3 ch, ch 1, sk next ch, **work a dec shell as follows: dc in each of next 2 ch, *yo, draw up a lp in next ch, yo and draw through 2 lps on hook,* sk 3 ch, repeat from * to * once, yo and draw through remaining 3 lps on hook, dc in each of next 2 ch (dec shell made), ch 1, sk next ch, dc in each of next 3 ch, ch 1, sk next ch, shell in next ch, ch 1, sk next ch, dc in each of next 3 ch, ch 1, sk next ch, repeat from ** across; ending with a dc in each of remaining 3 ch. Ch 3, turn.

ROWS 2 and 3 Work 2 dc in next ch-1 sp, ch 1, 3 dc in next ch-1 sp, ch 1, shell in ch-2 sp of next shell, ch 1,

3 dc in next ch-1 sp, ch 1, *work a dec shell as follows: 2 dc in next ch-1 sp, yo, draw up a lp in same ch-1 sp, yo and draw through 2 lps on hook, yo, draw up a lp in next ch-1 sp, yo and draw through 2 lps on hook, yo, draw through 3 remaining lps on hook, 2 dc in same ch-1 sp (dec shell made), ch 1, 3 dc in next ch-1 sp, ch 1, shell in ch-2 sp of next shell, ch 1, 3 dc in next ch-1 sp, ch 1, repeat from * across, ending 2 dc in last ch-1 sp, dc in end dc. Ch 1, turn. Fasten off at end of Row 3.

ROW 4 With right side facing, join CC in top of st at end of row, ch 1, sc in same st, ch 5, (sc, ch 5, sc) in next ch-1 sp, ch 5, (sc, ch 5, sc) in next ch-1 sp, ch5, (sc, ch 5, sc, ch 5, sc, ch 5, sc) in ch-2 sp of next shell, ch 5, (sc, ch 5, sc) in next ch-1 sp, ch 5, sk next ch-1 sp, *(sc, ch 5, sc) in center of decreasing shell, ch 5, sk next ch-1 sp, (sc, ch 5, sc) in next ch-1 sp, ch 5, (sc, ch 5, sc, ch 5, sc, ch 5, sc) in ch-2 sp of next shell, ch 5, (sc, ch5, sc) in next ch-1 sp, ch 5, repeat from * across, ending (sc, ch 5, sc) in next ch-1 sp, ch 5, sc in end dc. Fasten off.

ROW 5 With right side facing, join MC in first ch-5 sp, ch 3, sk next ch-5 sp, 2 dc in next ch-5 sp, ch 1, sk next ch-5 sp, 3 dc in next ch-5 sp, ch 1, sk next ch-5 sp, shell in next ch-5 sp, ch 1, sk next ch-5 sp, 3 dc in next ch-5 sp, ch 1, *sk next ch-5 sp, work a dec shell as follows: 2 dc in next ch-5 sp, yo, draw up a lp in same ch-5 sp, yo and draw through 2 lps on hook, sk next ch-5 sp, yo, draw up a lp in next ch-5 sp, yo and

CROCHET

draw through 2 lps on hook, yo and draw through 3 remaining lps on hook, 2 dc in same ch-5 sp (dec shell made), ch 1, sk next ch-5 sp, 3 dc in next ch-5 sp, ch-1, sk next ch-5 sp, shell in next ch-5 sp, ch 1, sk next ch-5 sp, ch 1, repeat from * across, ending when four ch-5 sps remain as follows: sk next ch-5 sp, 2 dc in next ch-5 sp, sk next ch-5 sp, dc in remaining ch-5 sp. Ch 3, turn. Repeat Rows 2-5 until afghan measures 55 inches or desired length, ending with Row 3. Fasten off.

Finishing Edge: With right side facing, join CC in bottom right corner of afghan, ch 5, sc in next ch-1 sp, ch 5, (sc, ch 5, sc) in base of shell, *ch 5, (sc, ch 5, sc) in next ch-1 sp, ch 5, (sc, ch 5, sc, ch 5, sc) in next ch-3 sp, ch 5, (sc, ch 5, sc) in next ch-1 sp, ch 5, (sc, ch 5, sc) in base of shell; repeat from * across, ending ch 5, (sc, ch 5, sc) in next ch-1 sp, ch 5, sc in last st. Continue working along side of afghan, working 2 sc for each row. Continue working across top of afghan as follows: ch 5, (sc, ch 5, sc) in ch-1 sp, ch 5, (sc, ch 5, sc) in next ch-1 sp, ch 5, (sc, ch 5, sc, ch 5, sc) in next ch-2 sp of shell, *ch 5, (sc, ch 5, sc) in next ch-1 sp, sk next ch-1 sp, ch 7, (sc, ch 5, sc) in center of dec shell, sk next ch-1 sp, ch 7, (sc, ch 5, sc) in next ch-1 sp, ch 5, (sc, ch 5, sc, ch 5, sc, ch 5, sc) in next ch-2 sp of shell; repeat from * across, ending ch 5, (sc, ch 5, sc) in next ch-1 sp, ch 5, (sc, ch 5, sc) in next ch-1 sp, ch 5. Continue along remaining side of afghan, working 2 sc for each row. Fasten off. Weave in loose ends.

PATCHWORK BABY DOLL AFGHAN

Put all those leftover odds and ends of yarn tucked away in the corners of your closet to good use. Easy-to-knit squares will quickly come together into a priceless doll blanket for some lucky little girl this Christmas.

Materials: Number 8 straight needles and number 8 circular needles, small amounts of various colors of 4-ply worsted weight acrylic yarn and a tapestry needle.

Finished Measurement: Approximately 2 x 3 feet

Gauge: 4 sts and 6 rows equal 1 inch

Cast on 17 sts.

Basic Square (make 48)

ROW 1 P1, *K2, P2, repeat from * across. ROW 2 and all even rows P. ROW 3 K1, *P1, K2, repeat from * across. ROW 5 K2, *P1, K2, repeat from * across. Repeat Rows 1-6 five times. Repeat Rows 1-4 once more. Bind off.

Finishing: Sew squares together, six squares across and eight squares down.

Border: (Work each side separately; sew corner seams together last.) With number 8 circular needle pick up and K80

KNIT

sts evenly spaced along top/bottom edge (100 along right/left side edge). **ROW 1** *K1, inc 1, repeat from * across. **ROW 2** *K1, P1, repeat from * across. **ROW 3** *P1, K1, repeat from * across. Repeat Rows 2 and 3 twice more. Bind off loosely. Sew corner edges of border together.

Tulip Baby Afghan

Tulips are a universal sign of spring and new life — the perfect pattern for a soft, snugly baby afghan. Unlike many patterned designs that are only presentable on the "right" side, this one looks equally pretty on either side. Its reversibility almost results in two afghans for the work of one.

Materials: Four skeins (100 grams in each skein) of worsted weight yarn, one 24-inch number 8 circular knitting needle and two stitch markers.

Finished Measurement: Approximately 28 x 34 inches

Cast on 136 sts.

Gauge: In garter st (K every row), 5 sts and eight rows equal 1 inch.

TO SAVE TIME, TAKE TIME TO CHECK GAUGE.

Border: ROW 1 K3,

KNIT

place marker, K to within last 3 sts, place marker, K3. **ROWS 2-4** K every st, slipping markers as you work.

Tulip Pattern: ROW 1 (Right Side) K3 (slip marker) P to marker (slip marker) K3. **ROW 2** K across. *Note: Markers are placed to remind you that the first 3 sts and the last 3 sts of every row are always K in garter st for border.* **ROW 3** K3, P6, *(P1, K1) three times in next st, P12, repeat from * across to last 10 sts, ending (P1, K1) three times in next st, P6, K3. **ROW 4** K3, K6, *P6, K12, repeat from *, ending P6, K6, K3. **ROW 5** K3, P6, *K6, P12, repeat from * across, ending K6, P6, K3. **ROW 6** Repeat Row 4. **ROW 7** K3, P2 tog twice, P2, *(K2, yo) twice, K2, P2, P2 tog four times, P2, repeat from * across, ending (K2, yo) twice, K2, P2, P2 tog twice, K3. **ROW 8** K3, K4, *P8, K8, repeat from * across, ending P8, K4, K3. **ROW 9** K3, P2 tog twice, *K2 tog, yo, (K1, yo, K2 tog) twice, yo, K1, yo, K2 tog, P2 tog four times, repeat from * across, ending P2 tog twice, K3. **ROW 10** K3, K2, *P9, K4, repeat from * across, ending K2, K3.

Repeat these 10 rows of Tulip Pattern until 21 patterns have been completed. Repeat Rows 1 and 2 of Tulip Pattern.

Border: ROW 1 K across, removing stitch markers. **ROWS 2-4** K across. Bind off.

Finishing: Weave in loose ends of yarn. Lightly steam afghan with an iron.

ELEGANT AFGHANS

HEARTS & FLOWERS AFGHAN

Shown in color on page 8

CROCHET

This soft springtime afghan is made up of 43 pieces: 40 granny squares and three panels of double crochet with filet hearts and squares. The borders and flowers are added later.

Materials: A size G crochet hook; a yarn needle; 1680 yards of 4-ply worsted-weight cotton yarn in peach.

Finished Measurement: 46 x 58 inches

Gauge: In dc, 15 sts and eight rows equal 5 inches. One granny square equals 4-1/2 inches square.

TO SAVE TIME, TAKE TIME TO CHECK GAUGE.

Granny Square (Make 40.) Ch 6, join with a sl st to form ring. **RND 1** Ch 6, (3 dc in ring, ch 3) three times, 2 dc in ring, sl st in 3rd ch of beginning ch-6. **RND 2** Sl st in ch-3 sp. In same sp, (ch 3, dc, ch 3, 2 dc), *dc in next 3 dc, (2 dc, ch 3, 2 dc) in next sp; repeat from * around, ending dc in next 3 dc. Sl st to top of beginning ch-3. **RND 3** Sl st in dc and next ch-3 sp, ch 3, (dc, ch 3, 2 dc) in same sp, *dc in next 7 dc, (2 dc, ch 3, 2 dc) in next ch-3 sp; repeat from * around, ending dc in next 7 dc. Sl st to top of beginning ch-3. Fasten off. Join four strips, each with 10 squares.

Panel (Make three.) Ch 29. **ROW 1** Dc in 4th ch from hook and each ch across — 27 sts. Ch 3, turn. *Note: Turning ch counts as one st.* **ROW 2** Dc in 2nd dc and each dc across. Ch 3, turn. **ROWS 3-8** Repeat Row 2. **ROW 9** (Begin filet heart) Dc in 2nd dc and next 11 dc, (ch 1, sk 1 dc), dc in each dc to end. Ch 3, turn. **Note:** *Sk one st refers to either a dc or a ch-1 sp.* **ROW 10** Dc in 2nd dc and next 9 dc, (ch 1, sk one st, dc in next st) three times, dc in next 10 sts. Ch 3, turn. **ROW 11** Dc in 2nd dc and next 5 dc, (ch 1, sk one st, dc in next dc) seven times, dc in next 6 sts. Ch 3, turn. **ROW 12** Dc in 2nd dc and next 3 dc, (ch 1, sk one st, dc in next dc) nine times, dc in next 4 sts. Ch 3, turn. **ROWS 13-15** Dc in 2nd and 3rd dc, (ch 1, sk one st, dc in next dc) 11 times, dc in last 2 sts. Ch 3, turn. **ROW 16** Dc in 2nd dc and next 3 sts, (ch 1, sk one st, dc in next dc) four times, dc in next 2 sts, (ch 1, sk one st, dc in next dc) four times, dc in last 4 sts. Ch 3, turn. **ROW 17** Dc in 2nd dc and next 5 sts, (ch 1, sk one st, dc in next dc) twice, dc in next 6 sts, (ch 1, sk one st, dc in next dc) twice, dc in last 6 sts. Ch 3, turn. **ROW 18** Dc in 2nd dc and each st across — 27 sts. Ch 3, turn. **ROWS 19-25** Repeat Row 2. **ROW 26** (Begin filet square) Dc in 2nd dc, (ch 1, sk 1 dc, dc in next dc) across to last 2 sts, dc in last 2 sts. Ch 3, turn. **ROWS 27-38** Dc in 2nd dc, (ch 1, sk ch-1 sp, dc in next dc) across, ending dc in last 2 sts. Ch 3, turn. **ROW 39** Repeat Row 18. **ROWS 40-63** Repeat Rows 2-25. Fasten off.

Finishing: With right sides together, alternate strips and panels and sl st tog. Steam to shape. With right side facing, join yarn at any corner (draw up a lp, ch 1). Keeping work flat, sc around, working 3 sc in each corner and 1 hdc at each intersection. Sc in each sc around, working 3 sc in 2nd sc of each corner group. At end, sl st to beginning sc. Fasten off.

Border (Make two.) With right side facing, beginning at corner of one end, join yarn (draw up a lp, ch 3). **ROW 1** Sk 1 sc, sc in next sc, ch 3, sc in same sc, *(ch 3, sk 2 sts, sc in next st — larger arch made), (ch 3, sc in same st — smaller arch made); repeat from * across to end.

Note: *In order to come out correctly you may have to adjust the number of sts between large arches.* Turn. **ROW 2** Ch 3, sk small arch, *in 2nd ch of large arch (sc, ch 3, sc, ch 3); repeat from * across, ending (sc, ch 3, sc) in 2nd ch of ch-3. Turn. **ROW 3** Ch 3, *(sc, ch 3, sc, ch 3) in 2nd ch of large arch; repeat from * across, ending (sc, ch 3, sc) in 2nd ch of turning ch. Turn. **ROWS 4-10** Repeat Row 3. Fasten off.

Flower (Make two.) Ch 4, sl st to form ring. (Ch 6, sc in ring) six times. In each ch-6 lp, (sc, hdc, dc, tr, dc, hdc, sc, sl st). Fasten off.

Leaf (Make two.) Ch 11. Sl st in 2nd ch from hook, work one st in remaining chs as follows: sc, hdc, dc, 2 tr, dc, hdc, sc, sl st. Fasten off.

Large Stem (Make one.) Ch 22. Sl st in 2nd ch from hook and next 9 chs; ch 10, sl st in 2nd ch and next 7 chs; sl st in remaining chs; fasten off. Sew these pieces onto filet square of center panel as shown in photo. Weave in loose ends.

ELEGANT AFGHANS

BIG, BOLD BEAUTIFUL DIAMOND AFGHANS

A big diamond usually elicits a very positive response when given to an unsuspecting woman from an adoring man. After all, when set in a ring, this precious gem symbolizes a declaration of love.

A big diamond afghan made for an unsuspecting man by an adoring woman will also elicit a positive response. Gifts that someone makes are always extra-special. Whether you knit or crochet, these afghans are bound to please.

CROCHET / KNIT

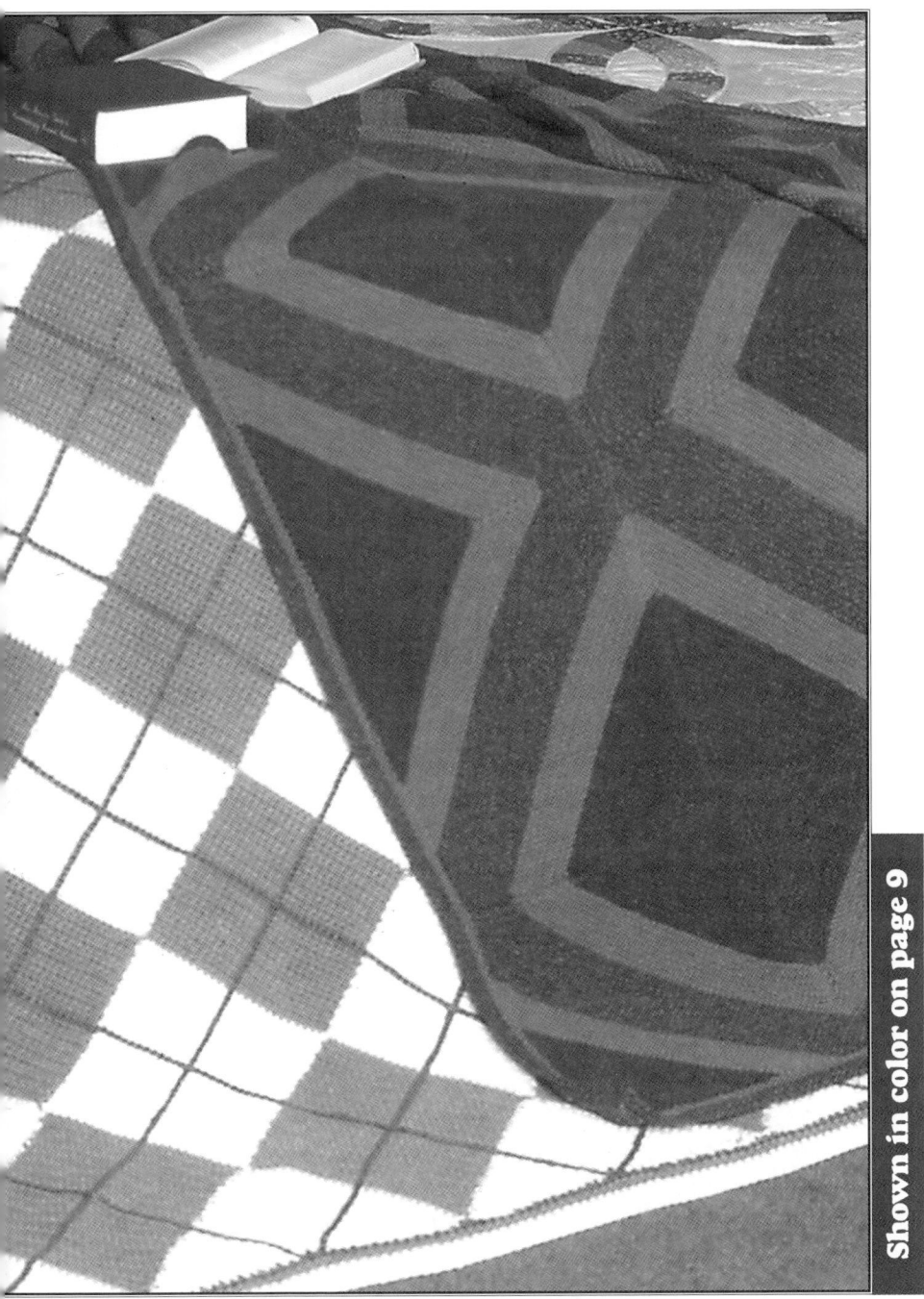

Shown in color on page 9

CROCHETED DIAMOND AFGHAN

Materials: Size I crochet hook; a tapestry needle; 4-ply worsted weight yarn in the following amounts and colors: seven skeins cranberry (A), eight skeins off white (B) and two skeins charcoal (C). **Note:** *Skeins should contain about 3.5 ounces — approximately 195 yards.*

Finished Measurement: Approximately 49 x 60 inches

Gauge: 3 sc equal 1 inch TO SAVE TIME, TAKE TIME TO CHECK GAUGE.

To make this afghan, strips of squares and triangles are crocheted, and then the strips are sewn together. The first strip is for the lower right-hand corner. Look over the diagram and read through the instructions for making squares, end triangles and side triangles to gain a basic under-

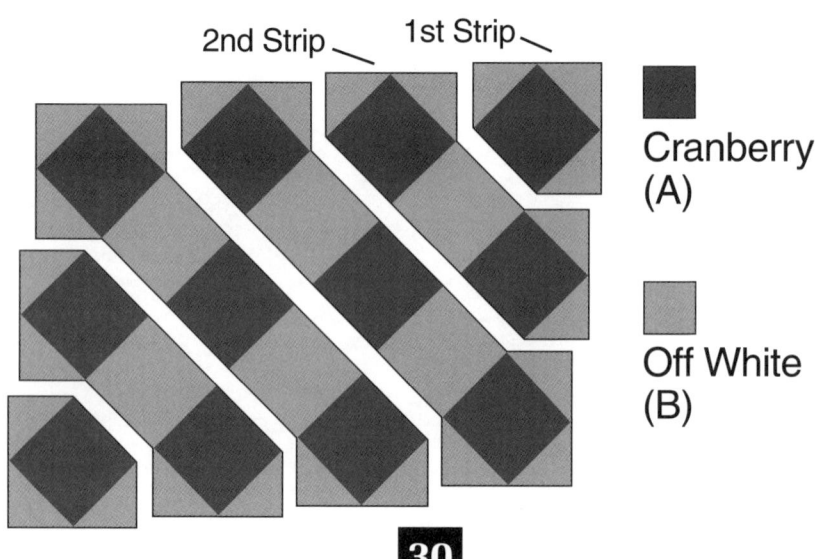

standing of how the afghan is made before beginning work on the first strip of the afghan.

Square: Ch 26. **ROW 1** (Wrong Side) Sc in 2nd ch from hook and each of next 11 ch, ch 1, sk 1 ch, sc in each of next 12 ch. Ch 1, turn. **ROW 2** Sc in each of next 11 sts, ch 1, sk ch-1 sp, sc in each of 12 remaining sts. Ch 1, turn. **ROWS 3-30** Repeat Row 2.

End Triangle: ROWS 1 and 2 Repeat Row 2 of Square. **ROW 3** Dec over the next 2 sts, sc in each st to the ch-1 sp, ch 1, sk ch-1 sp, sc in each st to the 3rd st from end, dec over the next 2 sts, sc in the last st. Ch 1, turn. **ROWS 4-11** Repeat Row 3. **ROW 12** Dec over next 2 sts, ch 1, sk ch-1 sp, dec over next 2 sts, sc in last st. Ch 1, turn. **ROW 13** Dec over first and 2nd sts, ch 1, sk ch-1 sp, dec over next 2 sts. Ch 1, turn. **ROW 14** Ch 2, sk ch-1 sp, sc in last st. Fasten off.

Side Triangle: ROW 1 With right side facing, place marker at middle of block edge. With B, work 12 sc to marker, ch 1, sk over marker, work 12 sc to end of block, turn. **ROWS 2-14** Work the same as for end triangle.

First Strip: With A, work one square, do not fasten off. Change to B and work one end triangle. Working on opposite side of beginning ch, work end triangle. With right side facing work side triangle on bottom edge. (See chart.) Weave in yarn ends.

2nd Strip: Work one

ELEGANT AFGHANS

square with A, do not fasten off. Change to B and work one square. Change to A and work one square. Change to B and work end triangle. Working on opposite side of beginning chain, work an end triangle. With right side facing, work one triangle on the bottom edge of first and last A squares. Weave in yarn ends. Sew to first strip as shown on chart. Continue working from diagram until all strips are sewn together. Weave in yarn ends.

Stripes: With C, make a slip knot. With right side of afghan facing you and yarn held behind afghan, draw up a lp in the first ch-1 sp in lower left corner, insert needle in the next ch-1 sp and draw a lp through the sp and the st on the hook.

Continue working in this way to the upper right edge. Fasten off.

Work stripes through each diagonal strip. For stripes going across the strips, work as above through the ch-1 sps of triangle then continue working across 15th row of each square to the triangle. Finish as above. Weave in yarn ends.

Border: RND 1 Join C at lower corner, ch 1, sc into the same st, work 16 sc sts along the edge of each triangle, work 3 sc into each center st, join with a sl st, turn. **RND 2** Ch 1, sc each st around, working 3 sc in each corner st. Join with a sl st, turn. **RNDS 3 and 4** With A, work the same as for Rnd 2. **RNDS 5 - 9** With B, repeat Rnd 2. Fasten off. Weave in ends.

KNIT DIAMOND AFGHAN

This simple afghan is perfect for beginners, or anyone else who likes to knit but hates complicated directions. This afghan is knit diagonally in garter stitch and is made of three colors in 24 individual squares. The arrangement of the squares is what creates the bold, geometric design.

Materials: A 29-inch number 10 circular knitting needle (or the size needed to meet gauge); a tapestry needle; worsted weight wool yarn in the following colors and amounts: 1305 yards blue (A); 1305 yards wine (B) and 1740 yards rose (C). *Note: Skeins, hanks or cones should each contain about 200 grams — approximately 435 yards.*

Finished Measurement:

☐ Blue (A)

■ Wine (B)

■ Rose (C)

·ELEGANT·
AFGHANS

52 x 82 inches

Gauge: On number 10 needles, 9 sts equal 2 inches

TO SAVE TIME, TAKE TIME TO CHECK GAUGE.

Note: *The 24 squares in this afghan are made entirely in garter stitch (knit every row) and are worked diagonally. The squares are sewn together with tapestry needle and yarn and the edging is worked last.*

Special Abbreviations:
Inc 1: Knit into the front and back of the stitch. **SSK (slip, slip, knit):** Decrease on the second and third stitches of each row by slipping two stitches separately as if to knit to the right needle then knit the two stitches together through the back loops.

With A, cast on 2 sts. **ROW 1** K1, inc 1. **ROW 2** K1, inc 1, K across. **ROWS 3-42** Repeat Row 2 — 44 sts at end of Row 42. Drop A. **ROWS 43-58** With B, repeat Row 2 — 60 sts at end of Row 58. Drop B. **ROWS 59-70** With C, repeat Row 2 — 72 sts at end of Row 70. **ROWS 71 and 72** K. **ROW 73** K1, SSK, K across. **ROWS 74-84** Repeat Row 73 — 60 sts at end of Row 84. Drop C. **ROWS 85-100** With B, repeat Row 73 — 44 sts at end of Row 100. Drop B. **ROWS 101-142** With A, repeat Row 73 — 2 sts at end of Row 142. **ROW 143** SSK; draw yarn through remaining stitch as if binding off.

Make 23 additional squares in the same manner.

Finishing: Sew all blocks together matching colors and pattern according to the diagram. Work in all loose ends of yarn.

Edging: The edging is worked one side at a time. Instructions are given for top and bottom edges with changes for the sides in parentheses.

With circular needle and B, pick up 146(225) sts. **ROW 1** K across. **ROW 2** Inc 1, K to within last 2 sts, inc 1, K1. **ROW 3** P1, K to within last st, P1. Cut color B. With C repeat Rows 2 and 3 three times (there will be 5 garter ridges in edging). Bind off loosely. Repeat on all sides. Sew mitered edges together with tapestry needle and yarn. Work in loose ends of yarn.

SEASCAPE AFGHAN

Pretty on a garden bench for porch or patio, this breezy looking afghan will remind you of the foamy waves of the seashore.

Worked in shell stitch and shades of blue and green, this afghan takes on the apperance of rippling ocean waves.

Materials: A size J crochet hook; worsted weight yarn in the following colors and amounts: four skeins each of bright blue (A), pale blue (B) and misty green (C).

Finished Measurements: Approximately 40 x 55 inches

CROCHET

Shown in color on page 9

Gauge: 1 repeat (14 sts) equals 4 rows; Rows 3-5 equal 1-1/2 inches.
TO SAVE TIME, TAKE TIME TO CHECK GAUGE.

With A, ch 136.

ROW 1 Sc in 2nd ch from hook and in each ch across to last ch; draw up a lp in last ch, drop A, but do not cut yarn. With B, yo and draw through both lps on hook — color change made. Ch 1, turn. **ROW 2** (Right Side) Working in *back lps only*, sk next 3 sts, 7 dc in next st, sk next 3 sts, *sc in next 7 sts, sk next 3 sts, 7 dc in next st, sk next 3 sts, repeat from * across, making color change to C in last st. Ch 1, turn. **ROW 3** Working in *front lps only*, sc in next st and each st across making color change to A in last st. Ch 1, turn.

Note: Always carry colors up side of work very loosely.

ROW 4 Working in *back lps only*, *sc in next 7 sts, sk next 3 sts, 7 dc in next st, sk next 3 sts, repeat from * across, ending with sc in next 7 sts. Make color change to B in remaining st. Ch 1, turn. **ROW 5** Working in *front lps only*, repeat Row 2. **ROW 6** Working in *back lps only*, repeat Row 3. **ROW 7** Working in *front lps only*, repeat Row 4. Repeat Rows 2-7 until afghan measures 51-1/2 inches, then repeat Rows 2 and 3.

LAST ROW Working in *back lps only*, sc in next st and in each st across. Ch 2, turn.

CROCHET

Border: RND 1 Continuing with A and working in both lps, count ch 2 as first st, **hdc in next 2 sts, hdc in each of next 2 sts, sc in each of next 4 sts, hdc in each of next 9 sts, *sc in each of next 5 sts, hdc in each of next 9 sts, repeat from * across until 7 sts remain, sc in next 4 sts, hdc in each of remaining 3 sts. Now, crochet down side of afghan, working one dc in side of each row. Repeat from **. Sl st in top of ch-2. Fasten off.

RND 2 With right side facing, join C to any stitch. Ch 1, sc in next st and each st around, working 3 sc in each corner hdc. Sl st to join. Fasten off. **Note:** *Increase or decrease sc to make sure there is a multiple of 6 sts around.*

RND 3 Attach B to a corner st, ch 3, 6 dc in same st, sk next 2 sts, sc in next st, sk next 2 sts, *5 dc in next st, sk next 2 sts, sc in next st, sk next 2 sts; repeat from * around. Sl st to join. Fasten off.

ELEGANT AFGHANS

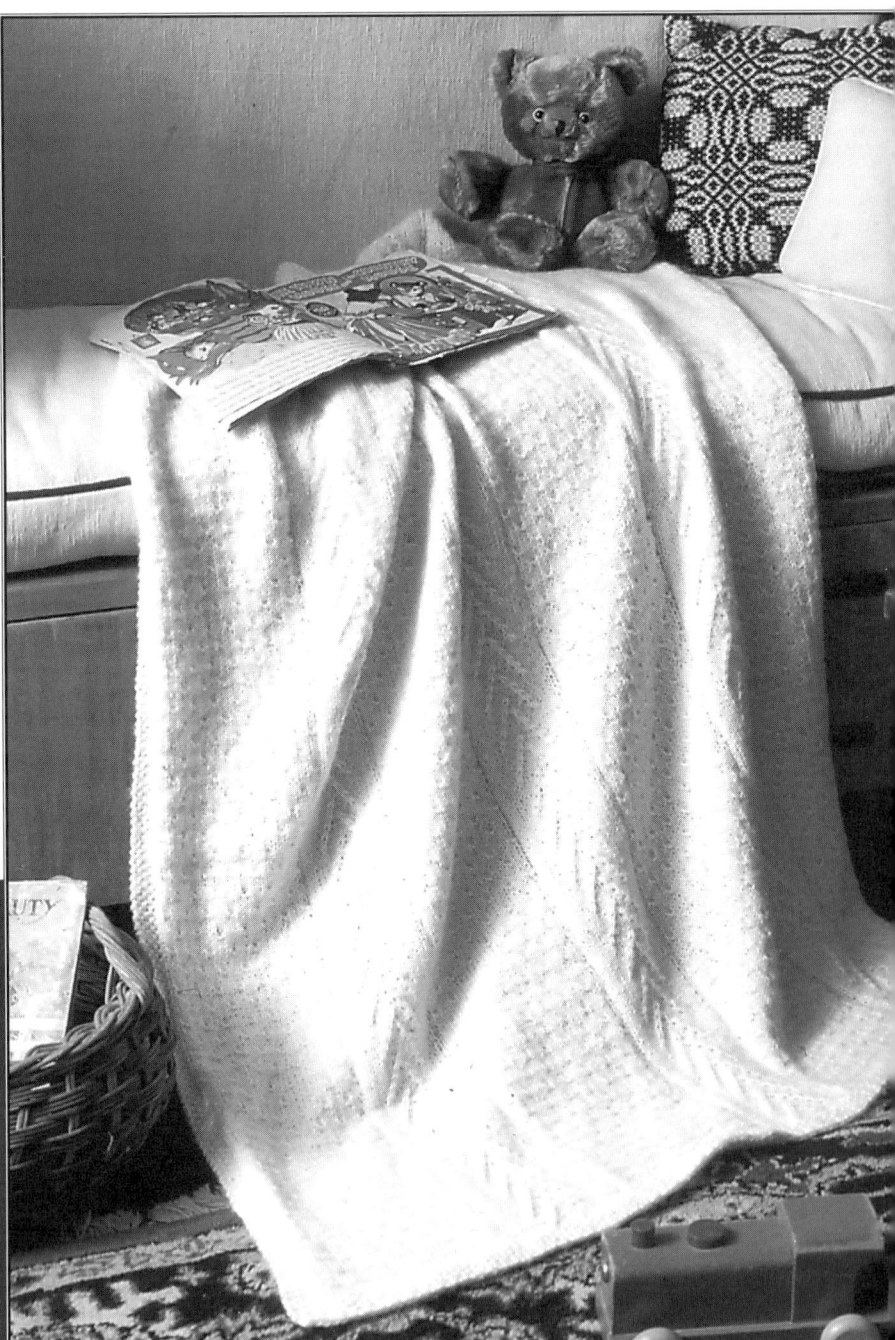

Shown in color on page 10

STORYTIME AFGHAN

Cool, cloudy days are good times for a child to curl up with a favorite book. This lap-size afghan is the perfect fit for a child. It will keep your legs and lap warm, too, when you're reading, watching television or doing needlework.

Materials: A 29-inch number 6 circular knitting needle and eight skeins of a brushed acrylic worsted weight yarn. **Note:** *Skeins should contain about 50 grams — approximately 135 yards.*

Gauge: In stockinette stitch, 6 sts and 7 rows equal 1 inch. Seed stitch panel is 5-3/4 inches wide. V-stitch panel is 4-1/2 inches wide.

TO SAVE TIME, TAKE TIME TO CHECK GAUGE.

Finished Measurement: 39-1/2 x 41-1/2 inches

Special Abbreviations:
Tw2R — sk first st on left-hand needle, K in 2nd st, do not discard from needle, K first st, discard both sts to right-hand needle.

Tw2L — Sk first st on left-hand needle, K in back of 2nd st, do not discard from needle, K in back of first st, discard both sts to right-hand needle.

PATTERN STITCHES

Seed Stitch: (multiple of 2 sts plus 1) **ROW 1** (Right Side) K1, *P1, K1; repeat from * across. **ROW 2** P1, *K1, P1; repeat from * across. Repeat Rows 1 and 2 for pattern.

Reverse Stockinette Stitch: ROW 1 (Right Side) P. **ROW 2** (Wrong Side) K. Repeat Rows 1 and 2 for pattern.

Simple Seed Stitch: (worked over 28 sts) **ROW 1** (Right Side) *K3, P1; repeat from * across. **ROWS 2 and 4** P. **ROW 3** K. **ROW 5** K1, *P1, K3; repeat from * across to last 3 sts, ending P1, K2. **ROWS 6 and 8** P. **ROW 7** K. Repeat Rows 1-8 for Seed Stitch Panel.

V-Stitch Panel: (worked over 19 sts) **ROW 1** (Right Side) K4, Tw2R, K2, Tw2R, K1, Tw2L, K

6. **ROWS 2, 4, 6 and 8** (Wrong Side) P. **ROW 3** K7, Tw2R, K3, Tw2L, K5. **ROW 5** K6, Tw2R, K1, Tw2L, K2, Tw2L, K4. **ROW 7** K5, Tw2R, K3, Tw2L, K7. Repeat Rows 1-8 for Panel Pattern.

INSTRUCTIONS

The afghan is made in one piece working back and forth on a circular needle.

Beginning at lower edge, cast on 185 sts. For border, work 6 rows of seed st. For afghan body, beginning with Row 1 of each pattern st, work as follows: 5 seed sts for side border, *28 simple seed sts, 1 reverse stockinette stitch, 19 V-stitches, 1 reverse stockinette stitch, repeat from * two more times, then work 28 simple seed stitches and 5 seed sts for side border. Keeping pattern sts established, work even to about 40-1/2 inches or length desired. End with Row 8 of the panel stitches. Work six seed stitch rows for border. Bind off loosely.

Sunday Afternoon Afghan

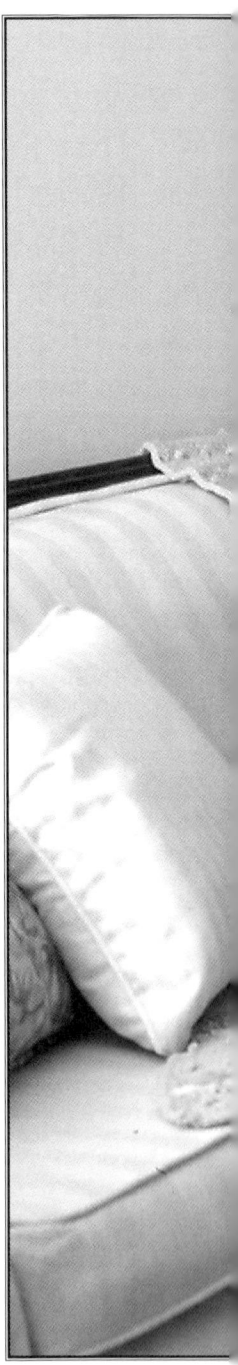

Sunday afternoon is the perfect time to curl up under a warm afghan and read the newspaper or a favorite novel. You can let your imagination take you just about anywhere in the world — from the safe and comfy vantage point under an afghan on your own sofa.

Materials: A size I crochet hook and worsted weight yarn in the following amounts and colors: 12 skeins beige (A), two skeins peach (B) and two skeins off-white (C).

CROCHET

ELEGANT AFGHANS

Note: *Skeins should contain about 3.5 ounces of yarn — approximately 173 yards.*

Finished Measurements: Approximately 46 x 66 inches

Gauge: 13 dc equal 4 inches

TO SAVE TIME, TAKE TIME TO CHECK GAUGE.

Special Abbreviations: p (picot) — Ch 4, sl st in 4th ch from hook. Note that this texture-adding picot lies between the single crochet stitches and is not counted as a stitch itself.

ROW 1 (Right Side) With A, ch 150. Dc in 4th ch from hook, dc in each remaining ch across — 148 sts. Ch 2, turn. **ROW 2** Dc in next and each remaining st across. Ch 1, turn. **ROW 3** Sc in each of next 3 sts, *p, sc in next 4 sts; repeat from * across. Ch 1, turn. **ROW 4** Sc in next and each sc across. Ch 2, turn. **ROW 5** Dc in next and each st across. Ch 2, turn. **ROW 6** Dc in each st across. Fasten off, turn. **ROW 7** Join B with sc in first st, sc in next 3 sts, *ch 3, sk next st, sc in next 6 sts; repeat from * across to last 4 sts, ch 3, sk next st, sc in 3 remaining sts. Fasten off, turn. **ROW 8** Join C with sc in first st, sc in next 2 sts, *working in front of ch-3 lp, dc in next st two rows below (Row 6), sc in next 6 sts; repeat from * across, ending with sc in 4 remaining sts. Ch 2, turn. **ROW 9** Dc in next 2 sts, *(ch 1, sk next st,

46

CROCHET

dc in next st) twice, dc in next 3 sts; repeat from * across to last 5 sts, repeat between ( )'s twice, dc in last st. Fasten off. *Do not turn.* **ROW 10** Join B with sc in top of turning ch, sc in next 2 sts, *3 tr in ch-3 lp three rows below, sk two ch-1 sps of previous row, **sc in next 4 sts; repeat from * across to last 2 sts (last repeat ends at **). Sc in last 2 sts. Fasten off. *Do not turn.* **ROW 11** Join A with sl st in first st, ch 3, dc in each remaining st across. Ch 2, turn. **ROWS 12-14** Repeat Rows 2-4. **ROWS 15-17** Sk first st, dc in each remaining st across. Ch 2, turn. **ROWS 18-144** Repeat Rows 2-17 nine more times. Fasten off.

Border: With right side of long edge facing, join A with sl st in corner. Ch 3, work dc evenly across to next corner. Fasten off. Repeat at opposite edge.

ELEGANT AFGHANS

POPCORN PARTY AFGHAN

Made with a size K crochet hook, you can pop this afghan together very quickly. It's the perfect gift from the heart to give to a friend or loved one for most any special occasion.

Please note that this afghan is made "sideways." In other words, you work the afghan from one side to the other instead of from top to bottom.

Materials: A size K crochet

CROCHET

ELEGANT AFGHANS

hook; a tapestry needle; 28 skeins of an acrylic mohair-look yarn in an off-white color. *Note: Skeins should contain approximately 50 grams; about 80 yards.*

Finished Size: Approximately 58 x 45 inches (excluding fringe)

Gauge: 3 dc equal 1 inch

TO SAVE TIME, TAKE TIME TO CHECK GAUGE.

Special Abbreviation: 5-dc popcorn — work 5 dc into next st, remove hook and put it into first dc of 5-dc group, replace original lp onto hook and pull it through.

Ch 179 sts. **Foundation Row:** (Right Side) Dc into 5th ch from hook, *ch 1, skip next ch, dc into next ch. Repeat from * across. Ch 4, turn. **ROW 1** Skip first dc and ch-1 sp, *(dc into next dc, dc into next ch-1 sp) twice, dc into next dc, ch 1, skip next ch-1 sp. Repeat from * across, ending row with dc into 3rd ch of turning-ch. Ch 4, turn. **ROW 2** Skip first dc and ch-1 sp, *dc into next 2 dc, 5-dc popcorn into next dc, dc into next 2 dc, ch 1, skip next ch-1 sp. Repeat from * across, ending row with dc into 3rd ch of turning-ch. Ch 4, turn. **ROW 3** Skip first dc and ch-1 sp, *dc into next 5 sts, ch 1, skip next ch-1 sp. Repeat from * across, ending row with dc into 3rd ch of turning-ch. Ch 4, turn. **ROW 4** Skip first dc and ch-1 sp, *dc into next st, ch 1, skip next dc. Repeat from * across row, ending row with dc into 3rd ch of turning-ch. Ch 4, turn.

Repeat Rows 1-4 for pattern until afghan measures approximately 45 inches from beginning, ending with Row 4 of pattern. Fasten off.

Finishing: Weave in all loose ends. Add fringe, if desired.

ELEGANT AFGHANS

Shown in color on page 11

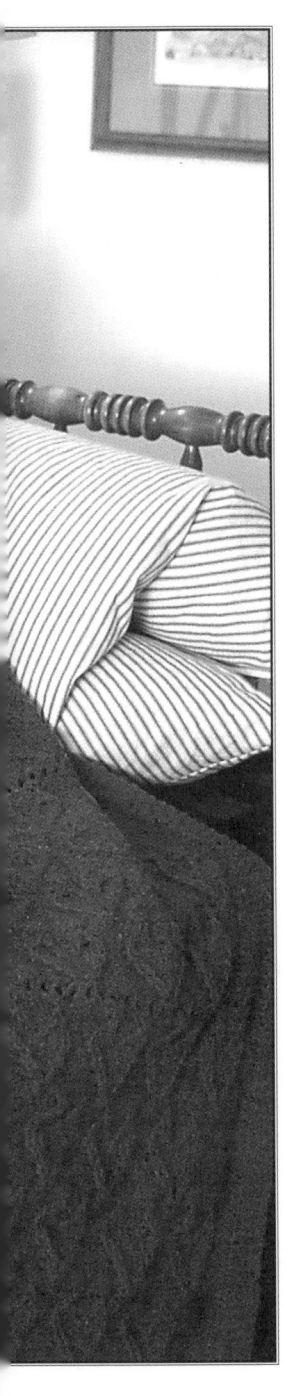

HEARTS AFIRE AFGHAN

This heart-adorned afghan is perfect to display a subtle message of love. The heart pattern is subdued enough that it can be used any time of year. It could also be a no-calorie Valentine's Day treat for that someone special you love.

Materials: Number 7 knitting needles; a tapestry needle; a cable needle; 100% wool knitting worsted yarn in the following amounts and colors: eight skeins scarlet red and one skein dark blue. **Note:** *Skeins should contain about 3.5-ounces — approximately 190 yards.*

Finished Measurements: 51 x 56 inches

Gauge: In stockinette stitch, 5 sts and six rows equal 1 inch. In Body Pattern, one 70-stitch panel equals 17 inches wide; Rows 1-18 of Body Pattern are equal to 3 inches.

TO SAVE TIME, TAKE TIME TO CHECK GAUGE.

Special Abbreviations:

C2F — K into front of 2nd st on left-hand needle, K into front of first st on left-hand needle and sl both sts off needle at same time.

C2B — K into back of 2nd st on left-hand needle, K into front of first st on left-hand needle and sl both sts off needle at same time.

T2B — Sl next st on left-hand needle onto cable needle and hold at back of work, K next st from left-hand needle, then P st from cable needle.

T2F — Sl next st on left-hand needle onto cable needle and hold at front of work, P next st from left-hand needle, then K st from cable needle.

m1 (make 1) — Insert left-hand needle from front to back into the horizontal strand between last st worked and the first st on left-hand needle. K this st through the back lp.

tbl (through the back loop) — work st(s) through the back lp(s).

PATTERN STITCHES

Garter Stitch: Knit

every row.

Eyelet Pattern: *K2 tog, yo; repeat from * across.

Body Pattern: (a multiple of 14 sts plus 4 sts; a repeat of 32 rows) **ROW 1** (Wrong Side) K. **ROW 2** P. **ROW 3** K8, P2; *K12, P2; repeat from * to last 8 sts, K8. **ROW 4** P7, C2F, C2B, *P10, C2F, C2B; repeat from * across to last 7 sts, P7. **ROW 5** K7, P4; *K10, P4; repeat from * to last 7 sts, K7. **ROW 6** P6, C2F, K2, C2B; *P8, C2F, K2, C2B; repeat from * across to last 6 sts, P6. **ROW 7** K6, P6; *K8, P6; repeat from * across to last 6 sts, K6. **ROW 8** P5, C2F, K4, C2B; *P6, C2F, K4, C2B; repeat from * to last 5 sts, P5. **ROW 9** K5, P8; *K6, P8; repeat from * to last 5 sts, K5. **ROW 10** P4; *C2F, K6, C2B, P4; repeat from * across. **ROW 11** K4; *P10, K4; repeat from * across. **ROW 12** P4; *K3, T2B, T2F, K3, P4; repeat from * across. **ROW 13** K4; *P4, K2, P4, K4; repeat from * across. **ROW 14** P4; *T2F, T2B, P2, T2F, T2B, P4; repeat from * across. **ROW 15** K5, P2, K4, P2; *K6, P2, K4, P2; repeat from * to last 5 sts, K5. **ROW 16** P5, m1, K2 tog tbl, P4, K2 tog, m1; *P6, m1, K2 tog tbl, P4, K2 tog, m1; repeat from * to last 5 sts, P5. **ROW 17** K. **ROW 18** P. **ROW 19** K15, P2, (K12, P2) twice, K15. **ROW 20** P14, C2F, C2B, (P10,

ELEGANT AFGHANS

C2F, C2B) twice, P14. **ROW 21** K14, P4, (K10, P4) twice, K14. **ROW 22** P13, C2F, K2, C2B, (P8, C2F, K2, C2B) twice, P13. **ROW 23** K13, P6, (K8, P6) twice, K13. **ROW 24** P12, C2F, K4, C2B, (P6, C2F, K4, C2B) twice, P12. **ROW 25** K12, P8, (K6, P8) twice, K12. **ROW 26** P11, (C2F, K6, C2B, P4) three times, P7. **ROW 27** K11, (P10, K4) three times, K7. **ROW 28** P11, (K3, T2B, T2F, K3, P4) three times, P7. **ROW 29** K11, (P4, K2, P4, K4) three times, K7. **ROW 30** P11, (T2F, T2B, P2, T2F, T2B, P4) three times, P7. **ROW 31** K12, P2, K4, P2, (K6, P2, K4, P2) twice, K12. **ROW 32** P12, m1, K2 tog tbl, P4, K2 tog, m1, (P6, m1, K2 tog tbl, P4, K2 tog, m1) twice, P12.

DIRECTIONS

Panel: (Make three.) With scarlet red yarn, cast on 70 sts. **ROWS 1-9** K. **ROW 10** (Eyelet Row) K5, *yo, K2 tog; repeat from * across to last 5 sts, K5. **ROW 11** K5, P each st and yo across to last 5 sts, K5. **ROWS 12-76** Keeping first and last 5 sts along each row in garter st, work Rows 1-32 of Body Pattern twice. **ROW 77** K. **ROW 78** K5, P across to last 5 sts, K5. **ROW 79** Repeat Row 10. **ROW 80** Repeat Row 11.

Repeat Rows 1-80 three more times. Then, repeat Rows 1-9 once. Loosely bind off all sts knit-wise.

KNIT

Finishing: With a strand of scarlet red yarn threaded into yarn needle, join panels together. Using a strand of blue yarn threaded into yarn needle, whip stitch around each of 2 center hearts in each "box" on center panel.

Border: (Make two.) With blue yarn, cast on 6 sts. **ROWS 1, 2 and 3** K6. **ROW 4** (Wrong Side) Cast on 3 sts and knit across. **ROWS 5, 6 and 7** K9. **ROW 8** Cast on 3 sts and knit across. **ROWS 9, 11, 13, 14 and 15** K12. **ROWS 10 and 12** P12. **ROW 16** Bind off first 3 sts and K across. **ROWS 17, 18 and 19** K9. **ROW 20** Bind off first 3 sts and K across. Repeat Rows 1-20 for 17 total times. K one row. Bind off all sts. With scarlet red yarn threaded into yarn needle and the right side of border facing, make a cross stitch in each stockinette stitch section of border. With scarlet red yarn and yarn needle, join border to lower edge. Make 2nd border as for first and join to opposite edge of afghan. Weave in loose ends.

ELEGANT AFGHANS

Shown in color on page 12

Sweetheart Afghan

This ruffly afghan makes a heart-warming addition to a bedroom decor. Make one for Valentine's Day and if your sweetie isn't in a romantic mood, you can always curl up with a good romance novel and a box of chocolates.

Materials: A size I crochet hook; a tapestry needle; worsted weight yarn in the following amounts and colors: 11 skeins red and four skeins white. *Note: Skeins should contain about 3.5 ounces of yarn.*

Heart Motif: (Make 39.) With red, ch 4. Sl st in first ch to form ring. **RND 1** Ch 5 (counts as dc, ch 2), (3 dc in ring, ch 2) three times, 2 dc in ring, join with sl st in 3rd ch of beginning ch-5 — 12 dc. For each rnd, do not turn. **RND 2** Ch 3, *(2 dc, ch 3, 2 dc) in ch-2 sp, dc in each of next 3 dc, repeat from * around, ending with dc in next 2 dc, join with sl st in 3rd ch of beginning ch-3 — 28 dc. **RND 3** (Forms Curves of Heart) Sl st in each of next 2 dc, sl st in ch-3 sp, * working along next side; sk 3 sts, 12 tr in next st, sl st in corner ch-3 sp, repeat from * one more time. **RND 4** Working in back lps only, ch 3, dc in each of next 7 dc; working in corner ch-3, 2 dc in first ch, sk next ch, ch 3, 2 dc in 3rd ch; working along next side, dc in each of next 7 dc across to the beginning of heart's first curve; working behind curves in sts from Rnd 2, 2 dc over ch to the right of sl st, ch 3, 2 dc over ch to the left of sl st, dc in next 7 dc of Rnd 2, 2 dc over ch to right of sl st, ch 3, 2 dc over ch to left of sl st, dc in next 7 dc of Rnd 2, 2 dc over ch, ch 3, dc over ch, join with sl st in top of beginning ch-3 — 44 dc. **RND 5** Ch 3, *dc in each st to corner ch-3, (2 dc, ch 3, 2 dc) in corner ch-3, repeat from * around, join with sl st in top of beginning ch-3. **RND 6** Ch 3, *dc in each st to corner ch-3, (2 dc, ch 3, 2 dc) in corner ch-3, repeat from * around, ending with dc in remaining 2 dc. Join with sl st in top of beginning ch-3 — 76 dc. Fasten off. **RND 7** With right side facing, join white in any corner ch-3 sp, ch 6 (counts as dc, ch

3), dc in same sp, *ch 1, sk next st, (dc in next st, ch 1, sk next st) across to next corner ch-3 sp, (dc, ch 3, dc) in corner ch-3, repeat from * around, join with sl st in 3rd ch of beginning ch-6 — 44 dc. Fasten off. **RND 8** With right side facing, join red in any corner ch-3 sp, ch 1, 5 sc in same sp, sc in each dc and ch-1 sp across to next corner, *5 sc in corner, sc in each dc and ch-1 sp across to next corner, repeat from * around, join with sl st in first sc. Fasten off, leaving 12-inch end.

Heart Border: With right side facing and curves toward you, working in unused front lps of Rnd 4, join B in skipped ch of Rnd 4 at bottom tip of heart, ch 1, (sc, ch 4, sc) in same lp, (ch 4, sk next lp, sc in next lp) four times, working across right curve; (ch 4, sk next st, sc in next st) six times, ch 4, sc in corner ch-3 sp of Rnd 2, ch 2, sc in corner ch-3 sp of Rnd 1, ch 2, sc in corner ch-3 sp of Rnd 2, ch 4, sc in first st of left curve, (ch 4, sk next st, sc in next st) five times, ch 4, sk next lp, (sc in next lp, ch 4, sk next lp) four times, join with sl st in first sc. Fasten off.

Small Motif: (Make 16) **RND 1** Work Rnd 1 of Heart Motif. **RND 2** Work Rnd 2 of Heart Motif. Fasten off. **RND 3** Work Rnd 7 of Heart Motif. **RND 4** Work Rnd 8 of Heart Motif.

Finishing: Sew squares together. Weave in and trim any loose ends.

CHRISTMAS TREE AFGHAN

Made up of several small squares, this afghan is great to work on any time there's a lull in your day. The yarn and crochet hook can be easily transported anywhere you might expect to wait — the doctor's office, the commute to work, or even while you're visiting on the telephone. You'll never feel like you're wasting time while your hands are busily occupied. Later, you can sew all the squares together at home.

Materials: A size I crochet hook; a yarn needle; worsted weight yarn in the following colors and amounts: eight skeins gray, six skeins green, three skeins red, one skein gold and one skein brown. **Note:** Skeins should contain about 3.5 ounces — approximately 240 yards.

CROCHET

Shown in color on page 13

ELEGANT AFGHANS

Finished Measurement: 57x63 inches

Gauge: Basic Square is 3x3 inches

TO SAVE TIME, TAKE TIME TO CHECK GAUGE.

Basic Square: With A, ch 4. **ROW 1** 3 Dc in 4th ch from hook. Ch 3, turn. **ROW 2** Dc in first dc (base), 2 dc in each of next 2 dc, dc in turning ch — 7 dc including turning ch. Ch 3, turn. **ROW 3** Dc in first dc (base), dc in next dc, (2 dc in next dc, dc in next dc) twice, dc in turning ch — 10 dc including turning ch. Ch 3, turn. **ROW 4** Dc in first dc (base), (dc in next dc, 2 dc in next dc) 3 times, dc in each of last 2 dc, dc in turning ch — 14 dc including turning ch. Ch 1, turn. **ROW 5** Sc in first dc (base), sc in next dc, hdc in next dc, dc in each of next 3 dc, (dc, 3 tr, dc) in next dc — corner, dc in each of next 3 dc, hdc in next dc, sc in each of next 2 dc. **Edge:** Work 2 sc in each row on side edge of square, 1 sc in corner, work 2 sc in each row on other side edge — 17 sc. Join with sl st in next st. Fasten off.

Work 68 gray squares, 70 green squares and 2 brown squares.

Work 72 squares with **ROWS 1-3** in gray, **ROW 4** in green and **ROW 5** in gray. **Note:** *When joining second color, leave length of yarn at start for use on edge at end of Row 5. When working with a second color, always carry first color in back of*

CROCHET

work and work around it. With gold, work bubbles over center st of **ROW 3**. **Bubble:** Pull up a lp around post of center st, *yo and sl hook under post, pull up a lp; repeat from * 3 times, yo and draw through all lps on hook. Fasten off. Pull end to back and knot.

Work 12 squares with **ROWS 1-4** in green and **ROW 5** in gray.

Work 68 squares with **ROWS 1-4** in gray and **ROW 5** in green.

Work two squares with **ROWS 1 and 2** in gold and **ROWS 3-5** in gray, leaving a 24-inch length of yarn at end of gold.

Assembling: Whipstitch squares to join. Join trunk squares. With gray, work along each side edge of trunk in sc for 4 rows. Follow graph to assemble tree and remaining squares for center of afghan.

Inside Border: With green, work 2 rows in sc all around (3 sc in each corner, 9 sc along side of each square). Join this and all following rnds to beg sc, ch 1, do not turn. Continue working in sc for 2 rounds each with green, gray, red and green. Assemble border following graph and sew to last row of inside border.

Outside Border: With red, work 7 rnds in sc (joining as before). Work one row in back st.

Finishing: Fasten off. Work in any loose ends.

AMERICAN FLAG AFGHAN

Y our support for the U.S.A. will be readily apparent with this American flag afghan. Make it with machine washable acrylic yarn and the afghan will be perfect for summer picnics and for gazing at fireworks on the Fourth of July.

The flag afghan is made of several granny squares, perfect for someone who dislikes working on large, bulky projects. A few squares can be made

CROCHET

·ELEGANT· AFGHANS

while watching television or talking on the phone — before you know it, you're ready to stitch Old Glory's look-alike together.

Materials: A size I crochet hook; a tapestry needle; worsted weight acrylic yarn in the following amounts and colors: five skeins red, six skeins white, one skein gold and four skeins blue. *Note: Skeins should contain about 3.5-ounces — approximately 245 yards.*

Finished Measurement: 52 x 64 inches

Gauge: Each granny square measures 3-3/4 x 3-3/4 inches.

TO SAVE TIME, TAKE TIME TO CHECK GAUGE.

Granny Square: (Make 49 blue, 75 white and 84 red.) Ch 4, sl st in first ch to form ring. **RND 1** Ch 3, 2 dc in ring, ch 2, (3 dc in ring, ch 2) three times, join with sl st in top ch of beginning ch-3 — 12 dc. Do not turn. **RND 2** Ch 3, dc in next 2 dc, *(2 dc, ch 3, 2 dc) in ch-2 sp, dc in next 3 dc, repeat from * around, ending (2 dc, ch 3, 2 dc) in ch-2 sp. Join with sl st in top of beginning ch-3. **RND 3** Ch 3, dc in next 4 dc, *(2 dc, ch 3, 2 dc) in ch-3 sp, dc in next 7 dc, repeat from * twice, (2 dc, ch 3, 2 dc) in ch-3 sp, dc in next 2 dc, join with sl st in top of beginning ch-3. Fasten off, leaving a 12-inch tail.

Stars: Make 49. (The flag afghan pictured is made up of 49 stars. To make yours more auth-

CROCHET

entic with 50 stars, you'll have to crowd them somewhat when positioning and sewing them on.) With white, ch 4, sl st in first ch to form ring. **RND 1** Ch 1, (sc in ring, ch 2) five times, join with sl st in first sc. Do not turn — five ch-2 spaces. **RND 2** Work (2 hdc, dc, ch 2, dc, 2 hdc, sl st) in each ch-2 sp around. Fasten off, leaving an 8-inch tail.

Finishing: Using long ends, sew squares together according to chart. Sew stars to blue squares.

Border Round: With right side facing, join gold in any corner ch-3 sp. Ch 3, (dc, ch 3, 2 dc) in same sp, dc around working (2 dc, ch 3, 2 dc) in corners ch-3 spaces. Join with sl st in top of beginning ch-3. Fasten off.

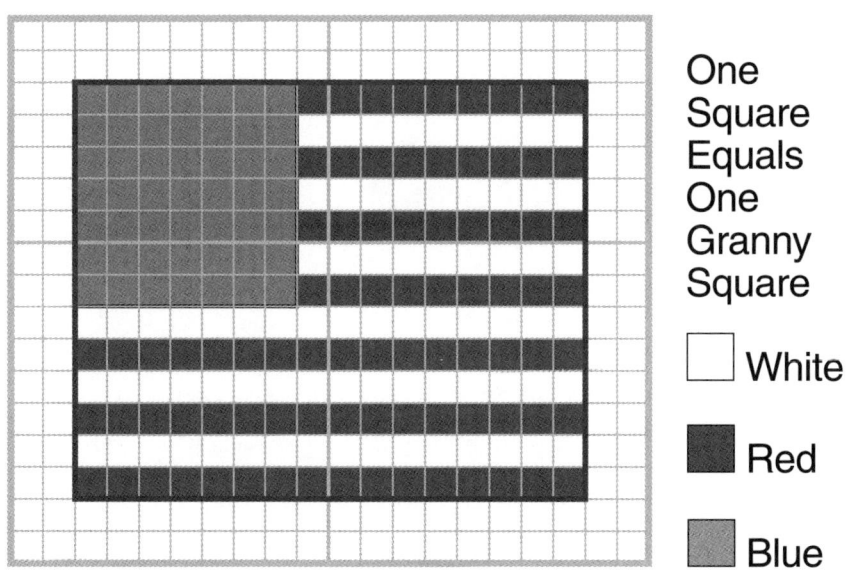

One Square Equals One Granny Square

☐ White

■ Red

■ Blue

ELEGANT AFGHANS

Shown in color on page 13

CROCHET

OLYMPIC RINGS AFGHAN

The design of this afghan combines the five traditional colors and interlocking rings that are the official symbol of the Olympic Games. The afghan is made of nine separate rectangles, five of which are bordered with one color. After the rectangles are sewn together, a border of all five colors is added for an exciting Olympic display. As a finishing touch, five sets of interlocking rings are worked and sewn to the single-color bordered rectangles.

Note: *The five interlocking rings are a trademark symbol. The design of this afghan is not intended to be made for resale; doing so would violate the Amateur Sports Act.*

Materials: A size I crochet hook; a tapestry needle; worsted weight yarn in the following amounts and colors: nine skeins white, one skein blue, one skein yellow, one skein black, one skein green and one skein red. **Note:** *Skeins should contain about 3.5-ounces — approximately 245 yards.*

Finished Measurement: 52 x 63 inches

Gauge: In dc, 3 sts equal 1 inch; 4 rows equal 2-1/2 inches.

TO SAVE TIME, TAKE TIME TO CHECK GAUGE.

Olympic Rectangles: (Make five — each with a different color on Rnd 7.) **RND 1** With white, ch 12. [Dc, (ch 3, 2 dc) twice] in 3rd ch from hook, dc in each of next 8 sts, [2 dc, (ch 3, 2 dc) twice] in end ch; working on opposite side of ch, dc in each of next 8 sts, join with sl st in top of beginning ch-3 — 28 dc. Ch 3, do not turn.

RNDS 2-6 Dc in each st to next ch-3 sp, *(2 dc, ch 3, 2 dc) in ch-3 sp, dc in each st to next ch-3 sp, repeat from * around. Join with sl st in top of beginning ch-3. At the end of Rnd 6, fasten off white. **RND 7** (Work Rnd 7 for each block in a different color. In other words, you will have five blocks when you're done: one with Rnd 7 worked in green, one with Rnd 7 worked in blue, one with Rnd 7 worked in black, one with Rnd 7 worked in red and one with Rnd 7 worked in yellow.) With right side

CROCHET

facing, join yarn in any ch-3 sp, ch 3, (dc, ch 3, 2 dc) in same sp, dc in each st to next ch-3 sp, *(2 dc, ch 3, 2 dc) in corner, dc in each st across to next corner, repeat from * around. Join with sl st in top of beginning ch-3. Fasten off. **RND 8** With right side facing and white, repeat Rnd 7. Fasten off.

Interlocking Rings: First Ring: With black, ch 16. Sl st in first ch to form ring, ch 3, 31 dc in ring, join with sl st in top of beginning ch-3. Fasten off.

Second Ring: With yellow, ch 16. With right side of sts on previous ring facing you, thread end of ch-16 through last ring made, sl st in first ch of ch-16 to form ring, ch 3, 31 dc in ring, join with sl st in top of beginning ch-3. Fasten

off, leaving 8-inch ends.

Third Ring: With blue, repeat instructions for Second Ring.

Fourth Ring: With green, repeat instructions for Second Ring.

Fifth Ring: With red, repeat instructions for Second Ring.

Arrange rings so blue, black and red are on top and yellow and green are on bottom. With long ends, sew rings to center of Olympic rectangles.

Textured Cross-Stitch Rectangles: (Make four.) **ROW 1** With white, ch 43. Dc in 5th ch from hook, dc in previous ch (4th ch), *skip next ch, dc in next ch, dc in skipped ch, repeat from * across — 20 crosses and 41 dc. Ch, 3 turn. **ROWS 2-15** *Sk next st, dc in next st, dc in skipped st; repeat from * across. Ch 3, turn. At end of Row 15, fasten off. With right side facing, join white in first dc of Row 15, ch 1, 4 sc in same st, sc in each st across, 4 sc in end st, work 29 sc along sides of rows, 4 sc in first ch of starting ch, sc in each ch across, 4 sc in end ch, 29 sc along sides of rows, join with sl st in first sc. Fasten off.

Finishing: Sew rectangles together as shown above. With right side facing, join white in any corner ch-3 before a long side, ch 3, (dc, ch 3, 2 dc) in same sp, *126 dc across long side, (2 dc, ch 3, 2 dc) in corner, 96 dc across short side, (2 dc, ch 3, 2 dc) in next corner, repeat from * around omitting last corner sts,

CROCHET

join with sl st in top of beginning ch-3. Ch 3, do not turn. **RNDS 2-4** (Cross Stitch Rnds) Sl st in each st to corner ch-3 sp, ch 3, (dc, ch 3, 2 dc) in same sp, (sk next st, dc in next st, dc in skipped st) across to next corner ch-3 sp, *(2 dc, ch 3, 2 dc) in corner ch-3 sp, (sk next st, dc in next st, dc in skipped st) across to next corner ch-3 sp, repeat from * around, join with sl st in top of beginning ch-3. **RND 5** Dc in each st to corner ch-3 sp, *(2 dc, ch 3, 2 dc) in corner ch-3 sp, dc in each st across, repeat from * around, join with sl st in top of beginning ch-3. Fasten off. **RND 6** With right side facing, join blue in any corner ch-3 sp, ch 3, (dc, ch 3, 2 dc) in same st, dc in each st to next corner ch-3 sp, *(2 dc, ch 3, 2 dc) in corner ch-3 sp, dc in each st to next corner ch-3 sp, repeat from * around, join with sl st in top of beginning ch-3. Fasten off. **RND 7** With right side facing, join white in any corner ch-3 sp, ch 6, dc in same st, dc in each st to next corner ch-3 sp, *(dc, ch 3, dc) in corner ch-3 sp, dc in each st to next corner ch-3 sp, repeat from * around, join with sl st in top of beginning ch-3. Fasten off. **RND 8** With yellow, repeat Rnd 5. **RND 9** Repeat Rnd 6. **RND 10** With black, repeat Rnd 5. **RND 11** Repeat Rnd 6. **RND 12** With green, repeat Rnd 5. **RND 13** Repeat Rnd 6. **RND 14** With red, repeat Rnd 5.

BLUE DIAMOND AFGHAN

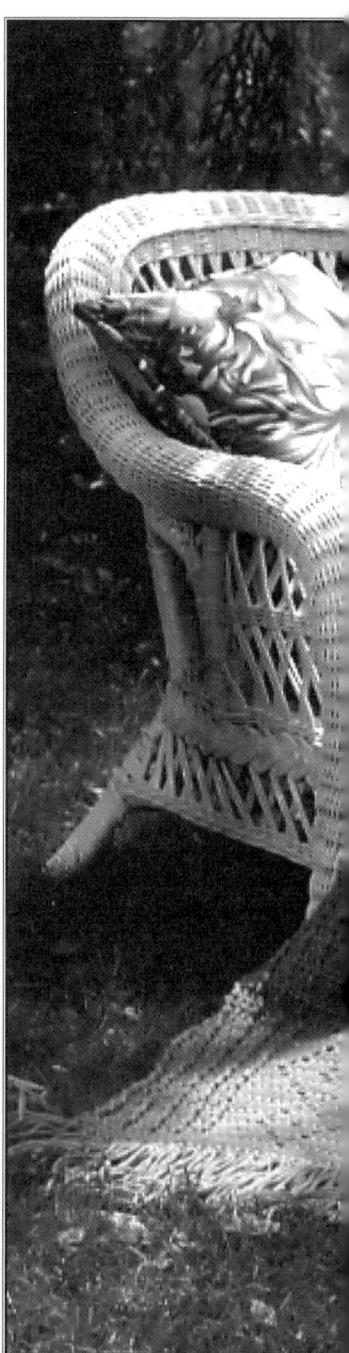

This pretty afghan's open diamond pattern makes it the perfect lightweight coverup for spring and summer.

Materials: Six 8-ounce skeins 4-ply worsted weight yarn and a size H crochet hook.

Finished Measurement: 66 x 47 inches minus fringe.

Gauge: 5 dc and 3 rows equal 2 inches.

CROCHET

Shown in color on page 14

ELEGANT AFGHANS

TO SAVE TIME, TAKE TIME TO CHECK GAUGE.

Special Abbreviations:
fptr (front post treble crochet) — yo twice, insert hook from right to left under post of next st, yo and draw through, yo and draw through first 2 lps on hook, yo and draw through next 2 lps on hook, yo and draw through remaining 2 lps on hook.

bptr (back post treble crochet) — yo twice, insert hook from right to left over post of next st, yo and draw lp through, yo and draw through first 2 lps on hook, yo and draw through next 2 lps on hook, yo and draw through remaining 2 lps on hook.

RTR Panel (Raised Treble Panel) — **For ALL EVEN ROWS:** (Bptr in next st, dc in next 2 dc) four times, bptr in next dc. **For ALL ODD ROWS:** (Fptr in next st, dc in next 2 dc) four times, fptr in next dc.

Begin Afghan: Ch 137. **ROW 1** Dc in 3rd ch from hook, dc in next and each ch across — 135 dc. Ch 3, turn. **ROW 2** Dc in next and each dc across. Ch 3, turn. **ROW 3** (Right Side) (RTR Panel, dc in next 8 dc, ch 1, sk next dc, dc in next 8 dc) four times, RTR Panel, dc in remaining dc. Ch 3, turn. **ROW 4** (Wrong Side) (RTR Panel, dc in next 7 dc, ch 1, sk next dc, dc in ch-1 sp, ch 1, sk next dc, dc in next 7 dc) four times, RTR panel, dc in remaining dc. Ch 3, turn. **ROW 5** (RTR Panel, dc in next

6 dc, ch 1, sk next dc, dc in ch-1 sp, dc in next dc, dc in ch-1 sp, ch 1, sk next dc, dc in next 6 dc) four times, RTR Panel, dc in remaining dc. Ch 3, turn. **ROW 6** (RTR Panel, dc in next 5 dc, ch 1, sk next dc, dc in ch-1 sp, dc in next 3 dc, dc in ch-1 sp, ch 1, sk next dc, dc in next 5 dc) four times, RTR Panel, dc in remaining dc. Ch 3, turn. **ROW 7** (RTR Panel, dc in next 4 dc, ch 1, sk next dc, dc in ch-1 sp, dc in next 2 dc, ch 1, sk next dc, dc in next 2 dc, dc in ch-1 sp, ch 1, sk next dc, dc in next 4 dc) four times, RTR Panel, dc in remaining dc. Ch 3, turn. **ROW 8** (RTR Panel, dc in next 4 dc, dc in ch-1 sp, ch 1, sk next dc, dc in next 2 dc, dc in ch-1 sp, dc in next 2 dc, ch 1, sk next dc, dc in ch-1 sp, dc in next 4 dc) four times, RTR Panel, dc in remaining dc. Ch 3, turn. **ROW 9** (RTR Panel, dc in next 5 dc, dc in ch-1 sp, ch 1, sk next dc, dc in next 3 dc, ch 1, sk next dc, dc in ch-1 sp, dc in next 5 dc) four times, RTR Panel, dc in remaining dc. Ch 3, turn. **ROW 10** (RTR Panel, dc in next 6 dc, dc in ch-1 sp, ch 1, sk next dc, dc in next dc, ch 1, sk next dc, dc in ch-1 sp, dc in next 6 dc) four times, RTR Panel, dc in remaining dc. Ch 3, turn. **ROW 11** (RTR Panel, dc in next 7 dc, dc in ch-1 sp, ch 1, sk next dc, dc in ch-1 sp, dc in next 7 dc) four times, RTR Panel, dc in

remaining dc. Ch 3, turn. **ROW 12** Repeat Row 4. **ROW 13** Repeat Row 5. **ROW 14** Repeat Row 6. **ROW 15** (RTR Panel, dc in next 4 dc, ch 1, sk next dc, dc in ch-1 sp, dc in next 5 dc, dc in ch-1 sp, ch 1, sk next dc, dc in next 4 dc) four times, RTR Panel, dc in remaining dc. Ch 3, turn. **ROW 16** (RTR Panel, dc in next 3 dc, ch 1, sk next dc, dc in ch-1 sp, dc in next 3 dc, ch 1, sk next dc, dc in next 3 dc, dc in ch-1 sp, ch 1, sk next dc, dc in next 3 dc) four times, RTR Panel, dc in remaining dc. Ch 3, turn. **ROW 17** (RTR Panel, dc in next 2 dc, ch 1, sk next dc, dc in ch-1 sp, dc in next 3 dc, ch 1, sk next dc, dc in ch-1 sp, ch 1, sk next dc, dc in next 3 dc, dc in ch-1 sp, ch 1, sk next dc, dc in next 2 dc) four times, RTR Panel, dc in remaining dc. Ch 3, turn. **ROW 18** (RTR Panel, dc in next 2 dc, dc in ch-1 sp, ch 1, sk next dc, dc in next 3 dc, dc in ch-1 sp, ch 1, sk next dc, dc in next ch-1 sp, dc in next 3 dc, ch 1, sk next dc, dc in ch-1 sp, dc in next 2 dc) four times, RTR Panel, dc in remaining dc. Ch 3, turn. **ROW 19** (RTR Panel, dc in next 3 dc, dc in ch-1 sp, ch 1, sk next dc, dc in next 3 dc, dc in ch-1 sp, dc in next 3 dc, ch 1, sk next dc, dc in ch-1 sp, dc in next 3 dc) four times, RTR Panel, dc in remaining dc. Ch 3, turn. **ROW 20** (RTR Panel, dc in next 4 dc, dc in ch-1 sp, ch 1, sk next dc, dc in next 5

CROCHET

dc, ch 1, sk next dc, dc in ch-1 sp, dc in next 4 dc) four times, RTR Panel, dc in remaining dc. Ch 3, turn. **ROW 21** Repeat Row 9. **ROW 22** Repeat Row 10. **ROW 23** Repeat Row 11.

Repeat Rows 4-23 four times.

Repeat Rows 4-11 once more.

NEXT ROW Dc in next and each st or sp across — 135 dc. Ch 3, turn. **LAST ROW** Dc in next and each dc across. Fasten off.

Fringe: Cut 14-inch lengths of yarn. Attach three lengths to every other stitch by folding yarn in half, insert crochet hook in stitch, pull folded yarn through stitch to form loop, and pull loose end of yarn through loop. Trim fringe if necessary.

ELEGANT AFGHANS

Shown in color on page 10

KNIT

Soft, Warm and Gray Afghan

Shades and textures give this simple knit afghan a classy look. Scalloped edges at top and bottom are mirror images of one another and attractive enough that there's no need to add fringe.

Materials: Number 10 knitting needles; a tapestry needle; worsted weight yarn in the following colors and amounts: six skeins color A (medium gray),

ELEGANT AFGHANS

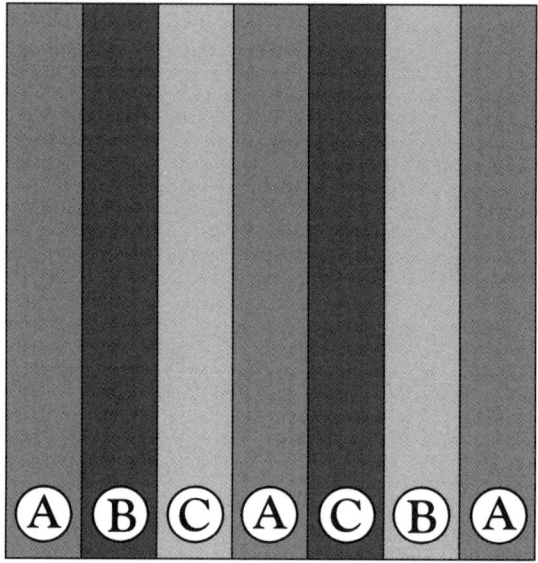

six skeins color B (dark gray) and six skeins color C (light gray). **Note:** Skeins should contain about 3.5 ounces —195 yards.

Finished Measurements: Each strip will measure approximately 6 inches wide by 5-1/2 feet long. Finished size of afghan is approximately 3-1/2 x 5-1/2 feet.

Gauge: In stockinette stitch (K one row, P one row), 8 sts and 10 rows equal 2 inches.

TO SAVE TIME, TAKE TIME TO CHECK GAUGE.

To make a strip, cast on 29 sts. **ROW 1** K2, yo, K4, K2 tog (twice), K4, yo, K1 yo, K4, K2 tog (twice), K4, yo, K2. **ROW 2** P across. **ROW 3** K across. Work these three rows until the desired length.

Make 2 strips each from B and C. Make 3 strips from A. Sew strips together.

INDEX

AFGHAN PATTERNS ALPHABETICALLY

American Flag Afghan (Crochet) 66

Big, Bold, Beautiful
Diamond Afghans (Knit/Crochet) 28

Blue Diamond Afghan (Crochet) 76

Christmas Tree Afghan (Crochet) 62

Hearts Afire Afghan (Knit) 52

Hearts & Flowers Afghan (Crochet) 24

Lacy Granny Ripple (Crochet) 16

Olympic Rings Afghan (Crochet) 70

Patchwork Baby Doll Afghan (Knit) 20

Popcorn Party Afghan (Crochet) 48

Seascape Afghan (Crochet) 36

Soft, Warm and Gray Afghan (Knit) 82

Storytime Afghan (Knit) 40

Sunday Afternoon Afghan (Crochet) 44

Sweetheart Afghan (Crochet) 58

Tulip Baby Afghan (Knit) 22

·ELEGANT· AFGHANS

Other Books From
THE CLASSIC COLLECTION

Collars to Knit and Crochet #3036 $6.95

Afghans to Crochet #3028 $7.95

U.S. State Quilt Blocks #3001 $9.95

The Complete Book of Jiffy Needle Tatting #53389 $18.95

Jiffy Needle Tatting, A To Z #53400 $8.95

Jiffy Needle Tatting, Quick & Easy #53397 $8.95

Jiffy Needle Tatting, Exciting Fashion Accessories #53419 $8.95

Jiffy Needle Tatting, Holiday Collection #53427 $8.95

More Great Afghans #53052 $9.95

Warm & Wearable #53079 $9.95

Lovely Laces (Large Print) #53060 $9.95

Boutique Bonanza (Large Print) #53087 $9.95

Stitchin' Time #53443 $9.95

Heirloom Quilts #5346X $24.95

Doilies and Dainties (Large Print) #53435 $9.95

Extra Easy Holiday Crafts (Large Print) #53486 $9.95

Use the coupon at the back of this book to order any of these project-packed books from the Classic Collection.

FREE PREVIEW ISSUE

Step-by-step patterns, charts and instructions for beautiful needlework projects, quick-and-easy crafts, tasty recipes, tips on canning and preserving fresh-from-the-garden fruits and vegetables, grow-it-yourself gardening guidance, tips on caring for houseplants and more! Send for your **FREE ISSUE** today!

❏ **YES!** Please send my free issue of *Flower & Garden Crafts Edition*. If I like it, I'll pay **JUST $14.95** for a one-year subscription (six big issues). If I'm not delighted, I'll simply write "cancel" on the invoice and owe nothing. Either way the **FREE ISSUE** is mine to keep.

One Year $14.95!

Name _____
Address _____
City _____
State and Zip _____

JBKS9

Complete and mail this postage-paid card to order your **FREE ISSUE** of *Flower & Garden Crafts Edition* today!

SEND NO MONEY NOW! Simply Mail This Card to Order Your FREE Preview Issue Today!

Your Choice

of One of These Popular Pattern Packets!

Free Gift!

A Whole Year of Fun Crafts
WBS1186

Plastic Canvas Baskets
WBS1071

Complete the order form on the reverse side of this card to send for your free pattern packet today!

Send for your FREE Issue today!

NO POSTAGE
NECESSARY
IF MAILED
IN THE
UNITED STATES

BUSINESS REPLY MAIL
FIRST CLASS MAIL   PERMIT NO. 2779   KANSAS CITY, MO
POSTAGE WILL BE PAID BY ADDRESSEE

FLOWER&GARDEN
Crafts Edition
700 W 47th Street, Suite 310
Kansas City, MO 64112-9839

Use this form to order your free pattern packet and to order other books from the Classic Collection.

Name _____
Address _____
City _____
State and Zip _____

Item #	Description	Qty.	Price
	Plastic Canvas Baskets or Whole Year of Fun	1	**FREE**
	Total for Books and Products		
	Shipping and Handling		$3.00
	MO Residents Add 6% tax, IA residents 5%		
	Total Enclosed		

Place order form in envelope and mail to:
**KC Publishing Products, Dept. B96
P.O. Box 11230
Des Moines, IA 50340**